To parents and teachers

We hope you and the children will enjoy reading this story in either English or Spanish. The story is simple, but not simplified so the language of the Spanish and the English is quite natural but there is lots of repetition.

At the back of the book is a small picture dictionary with the key words and how to pronounce them. There is also a simple pronunciation guide to the whole story on the last page.

Here are a few suggestions on using the book:

- Read the story aloud in English first, to get to know it. Treat it like any other picture book: look at the pictures, talk about the story and the characters and so on.

- Then look at the picture dictionary and say the Spanish names for the key words. Ask the children to repeat them. Concentrate on speaking the words out loud, rather than reading them.

- Go back and read the story again, this time in English and Spanish. Don't worry if your pronunciation isn't quite correct. Just have fun trying it out. Check the guide at the back of the book, if necessary, but you'll soon pick up how to say the Spanish words.

- When you think you and the children are ready, you can try reading the story in Spanish only. Ask the children to say it with you. Only ask them to read it if they are keen to try. The spelling could be confusing and put them off.

- Above all encourage the children to have a go and give lots of praise. Little children are usually quite unselfconscious and this is excellent for building up confidence in a foreign language.

Published by b small publishing
This new edition published in 2018
www.bsmall.co.uk
© b small publishing, 2000, 2018
1 2 3 4 5
All rights reserved. No part of this publication may be reproduced, stored in a retrieval system, or transmitted, in any form or by any means (including electronic, mechanical, photocopying, recording, or otherwise) without prior written permission from the publisher.
Design: Lone Morton and Louise Millar
Editorial: Catherine Bruzzone and Susan Martineau
Production: Madeleine Ehm
Printed in China by WKT Co. Ltd.
ISBN-13: 978-1-911509-69-1
British Library Cataloguing in Publication Data. A catalogue record for this book is available from the British Library.

Puppy finds a friend

Cachorrito encuentra un amigo

Catherine Bruzzone

Pictures by John Bendall-Brunello
Spanish by Thessa Judkins

b small publishing
www.bsmall.co.uk

Puppy wakes up.

Cachorrito se despierta.

It's Saturday.

Es sábado.

"Hmm…who can I play with today?"

"Mmm…¿con quién puedo jugar hoy?"

"I'm too tired," says cat,

"Estoy demasiado cansado",
dice el gato,

"come back tomorrow."

"vuelve mañana".

"I'm too busy," says cow,

"Estoy demasiado ocupada",
dice la vaca,

"come back later."

"vuelve más tarde".

"I'm too hungry," says horse,

"Tengo demasiada hambre",
                dice el caballo,

"come back this evening."

"vuelve esta tarde".

"I can't leave my nest," says hen.

"No puedo dejar mi nido",
dice la gallina,

"come back on Monday."

"vuelve el lunes".

"Come and swim with us", says duck.

"Ven a nadar con nosotros",
                    dice el pato.

But Puppy doesn't like water.

Pero a Cachorrito no le gusta el agua.

So he goes home.
Así que vuelve a su casa.

He plays with his ball.
Juega con su pelota.

He eats his lunch.
Come su almuerzo.

He sleeps in his bed.
Duerme en su cama.

"Who's there?"

"¿Quién anda ahí?"

"Can I play with you, Puppy?"

"¿Puedo jugar contigo, Cachorrito?"

"Mouse, you're my best friend!"

"¡Ratón, eres mi mejor amigo!"

Pronouncing Spanish

Don't worry if your pronunciation isn't quite correct.
The important thing is to be willing to try. The pronunciation guide here will help but it cannot be completely accurate:

• Read the guide as naturally as possible, as if it were English.

• Put stress on the letters in *italics*, e.g. *ag*wah.

If you can, ask a Spanish person to help and move on as soon as possible to speaking the words without the guide.

Note Spanish adjectives usually have two forms, one for masculine and one for feminine nouns, e.g. **cansado** and **cansada.**

Words Las palabras

lass pal-*abrass*

cat
el gato

el *gat*-oh

duck
el pato

el *pah*-toh

hen
la gallina

la ga-*yee*nah

horse
el caballo

el ka*bah*-yoh

cow
la vaca

lah *ba*kah

Puppy
Cachorrito

kachoh-*ree*toh

mouse
el ratón

el rat*on*

friend
el amigo/la amiga

el a*mee*goh/lah a*mee*gah

basket
la canasta

lah ka*nah*-stah

nest
el nido

el *nee*doh

tired
cansado/
cansada

kan*sah*-doh/kan*sah*-dah

busy
ocupado/
ocupada

okoo*pah*-doh/okoo*pah*-dah

to be hungry
tener hambre

tenair *am*breh

ball
la pelota
lah peh-*loh*-tah

lunch
el almuerzo
el almw*air*tho

water
el agua
el *ag*wah

to swim
nadar
nad-*ar*

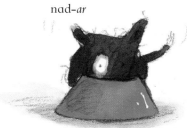

to play
jugar
hoo*gar*

to eat
comer
koh-mair

today
hoy
oy

this evening
esta tarde
estah tar-deh

tomorrow
mañana
man-*yah*-nah

Monday
lunes
looness

Saturday
sábado
sah-badoh

A simple guide to pronouncing this Spanish story

Cachorrito encuentra un amigo
kachoh-*ree*toh en*kwen*tra oon a*mee*goh

Cachorrito se despierta.
kachoh-*ree*toh seh despee*air*-tah

Es sábado.
ess *sah*-badoh

**"Mmmmm... ¿con quién puedo
jugar hoy?"**
mmm... kon kee-*en* p*way*doh
hoo*gar* oy

**"Estoy demasiado cansado,"
dice el gato,**
estoy demass-*yah*-doh kan*sah*-doh,
dee-theh el *gat*-oh

"vuelve mañana",
bwell-beh man-*yah*-nah

**"Estoy demasiado ocupada",
dice la vaca,**
estoy demass-*yah*-doh okoo*pah*-dah,
dee-theh lah *bakah*

"vuelve más tarde",
bwell-beh mass *tar*-deh

**"Tengo demasiada hambre",
dice el caballo,**
tengo demass-*yah*-dah *am*breh,
dee-theh el ka*bah*-yoh

"vuelve esta tarde".
bwell-beh *estah tar*-deh

**"Mo puedo dejar mi nido",
dice la gallina,**
noh p*way*doh deh-*har* mee *need*oh,
dee-theh lah gahl-*een*ah

"vuelve el lunes".
bwell-beh el *loon*ess

**"Ven a nadar con nosotros",
dice el pato.**
ben ah nad-*ar* kon no*sso*tross,
dee-theh el *pah*-toh

**Pero a Cachorrito no le gusta
el agua.**
pair*oh* ah kachoh-*ree*toh noh leh
*goo*stah el *ag*wah

Así que vuelve a su casa.
as*see* keh *bwell*-beh ah soo *kasah*

Juega con su pelota.
hw*ay*gah kon soo peh-*loh*-tah

Come su almuerzo.
koh-meh soo almw*air*tho

Duerme en su cama.
dw*air*meh en soo kama

"¿Quién anda ahí?"
kee-*en* an-da ah-*yee*

"¿Puedo jugar contigo, Cachorrito?"
p*way*doh hoo*gar* kon*tee*-goh kachoh-*ree*toh

"¡Ratón, eres mi mejor amigo!"
raton *air*ess mee meh-*hor* a*mee*goh